www.finishinglinepress.com

WATCHING BEES

NEW AND SELECTED POEMS

by

Michael H. Levin

Finishing Line Press
Georgetown, Kentucky

WATCHING BEES

NEW AND SELECTED POEMS

*To all the readers, critics and editors
who made these poems better*

ACKNOWLEDGMENTS

Versions of some of these poems originally appeared as follows:

"A Chorus Line," "Down by the Slaughterhouse," "Inheritance," "Ninth
Street," "Peter Quince Gives Up the Clavier," "Samson," and "To My
Grandsons, When You've Grown Old," in *The Raven's Perch*
"Above Sedona," in *Iron Horse Literary Review*
"Chicago," in *Atomic Energy Foundation Key Documents*
"Earth's Accidents," in *Scientific American*
"How to Read The Decameron," in *Mobius*
"I Am a Bullet," "Kunstovo," "Then There's the Moment" and "Watching
Bees," in *Rat's Ass Review*
"Noah's Wife" and "Troy," in *What Rough Beast*
"This" and "Kitchen Talk," in *Better Than Starbucks*
"Selektion," in *Beltway Poetry Quarterly*
"Steel Joy," in 2018 Anna D. Rosenberg Awards Collection (Poetica)
"Thoughts on Cezanne in His Old Age" in *The Federal Poet* and *The Spirit It
Travels: An Anthology of Transcendent Poetry* (Cosmographia)
"World Trade Two," in *The Federal Poet*
"What Is It Dies Today," in *Rat's Ass Review* and *Capitol Hill Rag*

Publisher: Leah Huete de Maines
Editor: Christen Kincaid
Cover Art: Kylie Baker, "Bee," Santa Cruz Island, Galapagos Ecuador (2018)
Author Photo: Becky Hale
Cover Design: Elizabeth Maines McCleavy

Order online: www.finishinglinepress.com
also available on amazon.com

Author inquiries and mail orders:
Finishing Line Press
PO Box 1626
Georgetown, Kentucky 40324
USA

Table of Contents

A CHORUS LINE

I never could high-kick
words were my tap-shoes;
but I know these dancers—

ecstatic routine masking terrors
of keeping on spot in the line,
self on the line; raw yearning,
stripped, on the line

those who sting most
departing stage left
in the husk of a grueling day

the one on the floor
silently screaming
felled by a faithless knee

Where do they go
what cold meal in a cold flat
their destination

disappointment
the price of dreaming

the awful question

When I can't dance
hanging like gallows from the flies.

ABOVE SEDONA
(In the red-rock country)

What eye can follow where these strata go?
Massed piñon branches stop sight as it flies.
The air is thin, and hikers must tread slow.

Unhesitant striations leap and flow
past canyoned pathways to each buttressed rise.
Few boots can follow where the rouge-red strata go.

Caprock grows porous that once wriggled, died
and rained like manna through pre-Cambrian tides.
The air is thin and travelers must step slow

yet pitch-pine embers by a fly-leaf tent
still glow. Our love is uplift and repose
though few may follow where these strata go.
The air is thin; and passion here moves slow.

CHICAGO

The Atomic Age began at 3.25 PM on December 2, 1942—quietly, in secrecy, on a gloomy squash court under the west stands of old Stagg Field.

What do trees know?
Their dead leaves scud
down Ellis Avenue, sodden
with snow: blown past steep gray sides
of a boarded-up stadium,
drifted in steppes on abandoned stands.

Cheers may come later. For now
tension snakes through the cube
of this court crammed with
its own cube: a ziggurat
of black bricks nesting cans
and control rods—fifty-some layers

inside square-timbered walls.
Tension; and fear. Fear of failure.
Faint terror of too much success:
reactions unchained like a
Frankenstein, rising and rising
in the old doctor's lab.

That's what they feel, hunched in
stiff wool suits on the catwalk,
fists jammed in pockets, puffing
breaths in the cold. Math is exact
but fission's still fickle; splitting
an atom seems dice magnified.

Yet it's science, not fiction:
no flickering bolts
just a needle on paper, scratching
slow upward curves. The leaves show
what's clear then: fruit plucked
or fallen cannot attach again.

DANCING WITH THE STARS

Three photos on a desk:
my mother at eleven, then age
doubled; then beyond. First frame, she's
effacée—long tutu held out
in a stop-time swirl, white coronet
perched carefully atop brown page-boy
bob, gazing with pride straight through
the shutter towards her father standing by.
Even my restless eye can sense
through sepia fade the pink intensity
of ribbons crisscrossed on her bodiced chest
and ankles fixed by wobbly chalked lines.
Can see the need enfolded in
her wavering smile.

Fast forward. Now it's Wartime
where she stands in Hepburn guise
between her widowed mother
and red-headed husband by
the thousand-dollar row home that they
bought in Thirty-Eight. He's taller
than them both by far—stiff-starched in khaki,
gaunt from basic; ready to depart.
The house will be let out till V-J Day.
My Nanny seems both pleased and
privately concerned: the slant light
catches worry lines along her brow.
My Mom (I think I'm born) is *en pointe* still,
a birdlike being poised, wired to fly.

The last frame shows her single in late
age—the larger house that followed
broken up, its contents and its sons
dispersed. Yet marks of time
are hard to catechize. Her hair's still dark
and coiffed, she holds advanced degrees.
The smile has broadened but remains
demure. Gone by are housewives' snickers
when she took flight back to school,
the snide remarks of in-laws

about disregarded place; her long-dead
sire descending dreamed Potemkin steps
to say that she'd done well.

                To see her
you must know that story line and read
the silences between its text:

an orphaned queen; the
furious protective drive to finish,
blaze, achieve—to carve as if with limbs
in air a space that's hers, though
milestones crush some tender
greens. But if we should be gifted with
full vision of that ballerina dance
in awe of sacrificial pain
we'd freeze.

DISCLAIMER
(A label)

This product was not produced
by harm inflicted on live
things: not animals or trees
or vegetables. We know that flowers
respond to speech and carrots
may contract when yanked from earth.
Beast or banshee, we respect
the dignity entire of
all created beings—bright-
colored, dun, or otherwise.

This product is not meant to
hurt your feelings, by intent
or accident. We know too
well from hard experience
how sensitive to slights each
fragile hope, each secret fear
remains. We would not cast harsh
shafts of light that shrivel your
sweet dreams. We just require a small
return to keep you warm in bed.

This product cannot
be a poem or play or
any type of art that glides
like scalpels through the skin
exposing shameful urgings deep
within. That driving purblind
horses to the brink, compels
them (though they buck and shy)
to drink.

DOWN BY THE SLAUGHTERHOUSE
(Babylon-Berlin 1929, Seasons 1-3)

In a trash-strewn
common courtyard
pig brains slosh round cracked white bowls
near a pail of blood whose level
slowly rises. Cleavers thwack,
while chained hounds lunge for scraps.

Mostly it rains:
beneath black umbrellas
surging in aimless rhythms
dark fluids slick the cobblestones
of foggy lanes, the vast flat plain
called Alexanderplatz.

Nothing is what
it seems. Our feisty girl detective
whores by night.
She's not her sister's sister.
The wraithlike therapist
may (or may not)

be our haunted
hero's lost brother.
A phantom fortune is (then is not)
painted coal. Undergrounds
sprout cellars; arrogant
puppeteers, new strings.

Corruption coils
through sleek salons
like whiffs of spoiled meat
as crowds break into manic dance.
What is real? Who is mad?

Meanwhile the
Crash of all things
civil looms.
          We need not linger
to see the baleful signal
blinking towards
our troubled backlit days.

DUMBARTON OAKS
(April)

Slim orange-blossom limbs
explode in white
against a tangled hillside
just beginning to remember
green. The brook extracts itself
from swaths of bramble
flush with riverine ambitions
as it spates past carefully-placed
boulders, lipping stone weirs.

This is the sylvan time
when finches purple up, curled
fiddleheads emerge, and weather
bunches and uncoils like racehorse
haunches as it nickers through
new leaves. When even artifice—
that master gardener's hand—reclines
beneath a cloak of flowering vines,
not having to deceive.

EARTH'S ACCIDENTS

The Dead Sea scrolls were mostly saved
by bribes and threats; unmindful finders
re-interred the rest in hopes of
gain. It vanished or decayed.

A trooper in the Greek campaign
blown by a Wehrmacht mortar down
a limestone chute, glimpsed there a lettered
chest—lost masterworks? new plays

by Sophocles, perhaps. Never
reclaimed: the next round covered it
up again. Fountains of blazing
loam, then forced retreat—the blasted

ground left no remains of site-map
to be guessed. Great Aztec wheels;
Lascaux' red bulls; dried funeral garlands
of Neanderthals—all brought to

light by restless chance: a dropped hoe
or a wandering goat. Vast evidence
unknown, we stand on ranks
of shoulders buried deep in earth

a fragmentary tune, made by the
breeze against a bone protruding
from a crumbled canyon wall.

HOW TO READ *THE DECAMERON*

It's all about Love—
sly, trickster, ravenous love;
lust, moved finally to forbearance
or peaceful restraint.

You must understand
they're avatars, courtly
yet coursing with hormones:
three rich boys, seven lady-girls

said to be Virtues
but red-lipped and flesh-bound:
besieged by the Black Death,
fled to a faerie landscape—

countering piled corpses,
suppurating sores, the stench
of pus from cloaked forms
stumbling cobbled lanes,

with dainty sweetmeats
set feasts by fountains
gay barcaroles. We know plague
better now: how it upends

expectations, extends
fingers of fear through cracks
and corners, turns beings to beasts
from quenched hope.

Half their town's defunct—
mothers, brothers, dukes
and clans swept away. Carts
trundle streets, stacked

with white bundles
yet the group chuckles at lying friars
judges in shit-ditches
wives clapped ball to buttocks

leaning on barrel staves.
What then, of the ending?
Casually, tales done, they
abandon their Gardens

return to a charnel-world,
untouched by fright.
By force of dance and laughter
charmed skies stay clear.

Their vaccine is story—
shared discourse of bawdy
deceptions, hot couplings,
transcendent friendship:

blithe band of humans
lambent in amber,
preserved by community
bearing sealed ampoules of joy.

I AM A BULLET—

no missile wings as straight
or with such fierce velocity,
humming in tune with siblings
from our chambered hive:
steel bees, swarming blued space
until we meet what dares dispute
our flight and bounce, transformed—

tumbling through livers
at compressive speed,
shredding veins; unseen
unless we carve an exit wound.
But don't blame me—
unchained resentment, black-clad,
was my baptistry.

INHERITANCE

I'm angry only . . . that he will have to relive my struggle with dystonia.
—*"Heir to Misfortune," Washington Post (2016)*

Turns out he's afraid
I'll get better and leave him
alone to suffer our disease.
So I said, gnarling the words:
maybe you won't play violin
any more. *But you can sing.*
And damn, right there, age ten,

he did. What fathers share with
sons cannot be captured live
for when he sang I felt my hands
unclench, a small straight pure
vibrato in my spine
revive. There's magic in these
gene cards that we shuffle out.

Some might say curse, though they'd
be wrong. We gambled when
we started off—they'd say
we lost. But as he sang
an emerald sea arose
and washed a beach.

We know, who
struggle now, the faces of
the monsters that we wrestle
with, and see as in dark mirrors
who we are. Through clouds
our glance is one more hidden gift
surprised: his copper hair; his
bright, too-wise, blue eyes.

KITCHEN TALK

Nobody told me
I'd inherit everything, all the ingredients—
anger and pity, grace with cruelty,
insight blurred by appetite:

a cousin's veined hands
pinching dumplings whose
spice she never disclosed

the great-aunt, once a softball star,
compulsively scrubbing dishes so
the next course can be allowed
(*What makes me so great,* she'd say)

my mother, fifteen again and furious,
eyes blazing past the tureen
because *they would not let me in*
when her father lay dying.

Near their tombstones
encroached on by ivy, sparse
cypress lean over standing water.

The recipes I'm bequeathed are meals
for fishes, splattered by spoons
and sauces, stained with secrets.

By their baking tins,
over the cutlery,
filaments drift
through simmering rooms.

KUNSTOVO

(5 March 1953)

They say Maria Yudina's recording of Mozart was on the
record player when the 'leader and teacher' was found...
—Shostakovich, Testimony (1979)

The fast-play disk
spins, stylus
scratching spindle.
The Hetman's defunct
though no one yet knows.
It's three AM; when
minions arrive, fearful
to knock, there'll be hell to pay
and savage successions.

He sprawls on
his couch in Red pseudo-garb,
short as a toadstool, webfoot
concealed by tall boots
nicotined fingers flung
outward; pockmarks for once
not erased. The disk

was made from pure panic:
hearing her broadcast, he
asked for the record—the
session was live. Pre-dawn

saw a terrified
orchestra, quivering
conductors, marched to fulfill
his 'wish.' One round
quickly was pressed.
When he sent her a cash prize
she gifted it whole to the Church
"For your sins."

Warrants to wipe her
lay blank on his desk
though millions were inked
without pity. Opaque

as Asia, did the ogre
have sentiments? Was it
merely a whim of power?
His cause held lives less than zero

yet she played on:
force steely and strange
to faint applause.

MT. ST. HELENS
(1982)

When the peak blew
I was takin a piss.
The trees went flat as GIs
at machine-gun drill.
We jumped in the trailer
slid two mile.

It was amazin—
the ridge tipped up
like jello. This wall of ash
boilt down the hill.
I never did get
my fly zipped. Sure,

we got out—they don't give
medals for that. But lemme say
when the wind stopped
I was holdin my nuts
in both hands.
Chuck shit his pants.

I got no hair to the left, an
that ear still hums
when it's quiet.
It hurts to think
a man can't depend
on nothin

even keepin his feet
on the ground
no more.

NINTH STREET
(Capitol Hill, November)

Behind this row of windows
squared against the snap of evening
air, light nests like coals. Repointed
chimneys plume their hellos. The dusk
grows soft with satisfaction
and collecting ash. Tracing
the embers' crack and fall, I do not
feel deep roots contract; trees thickening
their bark, expecting ice.

When the white coat
of winter splits, what season
will emerge? Spare me the irony
of being sucked dry by thirst.
Let me be poised and patient,
plangent as a guitar. Let me
absorb this golden haze, while day
declines and leaves quilt up the ground
against the dawn.

NOAH'S WIFE
(Chester Pageant Play, c. 1530)

After the stern command
growling with vengeance
her husband's meek salute
after the sweaty rush
cedars cut, planked, bent, pitch boiled
slapped on, grain threshed, provender
hauled; beasts lassoed corralled
driven lowing pissing rump-shat
up the slippery ramp

she declines to board.
You go, she says—*I'll catch up*
with you later. Here, see my friends;
we're not finished our wine.
Their tale's too good to miss.
Sons are sent serially—
Shem, Ham, Japheth. She boxes
their ears for impertinence,
annoyed at rude interruptions.
Finally, unhurried

but nudged by their haste
and scripture's iron script, she consents:
cantankerous female
with no name but Missus, stubborn
beyond reason—or a last
toast with others
more dear to her, delaying
the doom of an angry
male flood.

PETER QUINCE GIVES UP THE CLAVIER
(Wrong, Wallace Stevens)

If padded hammers striking
copper wires comprise desire
I find the tune grown thin. That
theme has faded into evening
air, deformed by metaphor.

The body is immortal
in the moment only, not
arpeggios. Parsed feelings
are mere puppet shows. Better
to drown oneself in touch

than float, still sighing, on green
garden pools, rehearsing more
and endlessly one's old
continuos. Better to
glide through thighs and breasts, plucking

chance strings or being plucked by them.
That melody resounds. So now
I'll shut the keyboard up and
go reside beneath the sign
of tousled limbs. And

in that sumptuous silence
kiss; be kissed.

RAGTIME
(After the death of our sled dog)

Tell me that joke again, Marse Death;
slip me the inside scoop on why
your painted laugh means mirth.
Extemporize anew your comic theme
of burdens lifted by releasing earth

wrapped in the two-step
of that old soft-shoe routine,
the tinkle of vaudevillian
dreams. Gone are my eager sidekick
and his amber gaze. I need a pick-up

but cannot agree that every kiss
begins a playbook of
good-byes. O interlocutor
supreme, strut by, black cane tucked tight
beneath one white-gloved arm. Your upbeat

pantomime gets poor reviews—doctor
that faded script, take out a brand-new
act on tour: it's spring, add bright
new tunes, the time is right for
artifice and magic shows.

Thanks for the invite, but I find
I must refuse. Though foxglove opens
and sweet larkspur blooms, that winter calls
and still I long to go, where fading
pawprints flatten in the slumping snow.

Where fading pawprints flatten
in the slumping snow

SAMSON

His problem was women, the
rabbis wrote later: seduction, betrayal,
snaky worming towards secrets.
Women, and borders—
lands where lived Others
no man should pursue.

His loves all were Gentile, they noted: ripe thighs
of Timrath, of Gaza; the Philistine princess
they sought to derate. In service to morals they
bleached out his lameness, his vast overcomings, this
riddler and teaser whose rage masked belief. They
skirted his violence—made bland

ripping lions, killing hundreds with jawbones,
tumbling stone gates on assassins in wait.
                                        Judging
is quick, though justice moves slowly. His flaws were god
weapons: A hot-eyed playfulness. The fierce
roving glance that leaped every boundary,
reveled in vengeance.

Let scribes sheepskin their worst.
His tale speaks liberating passion
not a poisoned female curse.

SELEKTION (1943)

Alexander Tamir:

So here we are, in the Vilna Ghetto.
Emptiness, everywhere.
Graves bloom like flowers, heavy with rain.
That's *'poetry'*—in Ponar
where the seized go, are no graves,
just palls of smoke, stinking the trees.

Because I'm eleven they think
I can't see everyone *waiting.*
They don't want that I see; but my eyes
record this corpse (stairwell),
that beggar (courtyard), the soprano
stripped naked to sing, before the shots.

No space is safe here. The Jerusalem
of the West has become something else.
You can disappear at practice,
going for bread, even with work permits.

If I live, I'll refuse
to remember this time that breeds hate.
I'll fight to forget, go on playing.
Though the song I wrote
may be sung now to weeping

it was a different beginning.

Alexander Tamir (1931-2019), age 11, wrote the resistance lullaby Shtiller, Shtiller ("Hush, Hush") for a Jewish Council talent competition four months before the Vilna Ghetto was liquidated. Its origins as an international Holocaust anthem and his return to Vilna 60 years later are recounted in the film Ponar (2002). He and his wife Bracha Eden (1929-2006) became the world's foremost classical piano duo.

STEEL JOY

(For Oskar Burstein, Petrograd 1922—Maryland 2016)

The scars that date to Luga
now are still; big hands that bowed
the cello, silently at
rest. Those other scars—from
famine, father, Siege; blind
GPU arrest, two camps,
an airless aftermath—
re-forged: cold-welded in
a steel determination
that the Headman must not win.
That song and blood ties,
pulses in a secret heart,
would not be waived.

And so all guests were family
at your table's toasts:
both those who haltingly
dropped by for fear of being
marked, and we who came there
later, late in life: the welcome
shifted to a foreign land that
was not strange—was home, because
you dreamed it all your days. Your
bear hugs and irreverent joy among
pink redbuds and magnolia flowers
a coda to the dark hard times.
A middle finger raised.

An endless chord.

STYX

The boat veers through shallows,
its only sound the bubbling
of slipped oars.

Bald-headed, snooded or beret'd,
shapes throng the nearing shore
close-ranked as stands of aspen.

Something erasive grays sharp profiles,
smudges the glint of pinky rings—a fog
of letting go, perhaps, or yearning;
eyes blank as eggs.

Pale faces turn
and as in breezes speak:

We are the last surprised.
Remember us when you break bread
or brush back a strand of dear
ones' hair; in the braided
burrow of each lovers' bed.

You too will be betrayed.

THEN THERE'S THE MOMENT

when the blade snicks your rib
the plane goes into a dive

your wrist severs the window,
spurting carnelian

an eighteen-wheeler hurtles
towards your windshield

you see there's no more to add
that this, right now,

is the summing up

THIS

What is this twinge,
this ache, this known routine
of how we scratch and cough
and clip our nails. The way
you fold your socks
and borrow back my shaving cream.
This truce of fixed points
and necessary distance.

This flash of eyes
that breaks and soars
like songbirds scattered by falcons.
This pause, this warm stopped bass.
This pulse in the night.
This love.

THOUGHTS ON CÉZANNE IN HIS OLD AGE

I could take in boarders
breakfast on crusts and water
drag sore knees and a jointed
German easel to the
rutted ridge near an
undistinguished hump
of brooding rock, painted
again and again

grow my beard wild as abandoned fields
if crazed pronouncements
came with that fierce cool gaze
caressing with infinite tenderness
the golden skin
of a perfectly
ordinary
peach.

TROY

When they crashed through the palace
the iron chests were empty.
It was all fatal illusion:
words, only words—the small
bronze-age fortress far from Mycenae
grown huge through tales told;
betrayal, greed, prideful ambition
enlarged by rhetoric,
tall gods and goddesses
gliding through battle,
deflecting spears, guiding them,
shedding bright ichor for
chosen-up sides. Plunder
soon scattered in quarrels
and bloodsoaked revenge.

Where are the phoenix-faced breastplate,
the greaves clasped with silver,
those thickets of ash shafts,
the horsetail-plumed helmet
that Hector once wore?
Where the thousand black ships,
the throngs of wandering dead?
What floats in our air
from that long, troubled decade—
plague, rage, endless siege
are scenes set in mental stained glass:

The lithe joyful daughter, lured
by promise of marriage, limp
on an altar in Aulis so her father
might sail. An aged king, fifty sons
shades or soon to be, come cloaked
alone to seek his heir's
mangled body for burial.
Achilles, Patroclus
coolly caressing
each other's doomed flesh.

Perhaps that's the moral:
love, just love, for all its fraught twists
and sad endings, is the sole
godlike strand of us—transcendent
in passion or comradeship;
conserving what honor
flawed selves may possess.

TO MY GRANDSONS, WHEN YOU'VE GROWN OLD

If you read this then
you barely may remember me:
a whisper; two notes from the span
of my voice—perhaps a shadow picture
of the way I cuddled in your beds
at night reading the last lines
of your evening books, confused with
images from photographs.

I wished you life—a long one
if it please, with all the healed-up
losses and accomplishments
of silent existential faith.
I hope that part of what remains
when pain assaults your knees
or disappointments in career or love
or choices that your children make arise

is that warm aura when the moon came up
and silvered your smooth bodies
and the lovely outlines of your
thick-lashed sleeping heads.

WALKING

(For Eli Ginzberg, 1906-2002)

So there we were, stumping the shore again:
gulls brooming the air, a mackerel-
fisted osprey thumping above, damp sand
lapsing into itself

you in your long-billed cap,
frayed beach-wrap trailing
like a coronation robe

me with my annual load
of half-done deeds,
hands thrust in pockets

an odd pair, four decades different,
edging towards sunset on unsteady
footing. Foam crossed our shadows;
plovers typed out patterns in that sheen.

The game was discourse—searching
as sabers, unroofing root cellars,
exploding foundations
despite our forbidding grandfathers

your white moustache gleaming
head erect against the mares-tails
as dusk walked down the wrack line
and tides turned pewter with banked fire.

WATCHING BEES

I'm looking at a bee
dance slowly to its compass
through the thrust-out leaves
of cherry trees that drop
pink double blossoms
on a dusty asphalt drive.

Patched fellow, he's not
looking at me. Diverging, all
furred purpose, see him bumble
to the next browned bloom,
mapping the day's descent from
branch to flowering shrub

to plump red tulip lips
that pucker up below. Comes now the
falling time we thoughtlessly
call spring, when petals open
then proceed to desiccate
and die. When pollen folk

make haste to seize the last
sweet drip or crumb, alive
to ticking landscapes,
to accelerating sun.
                    I'm looking
at a me who's disregarded by
a bee. Whose eye sees less

acutely, seeking out a
hive. Who lacks the surefoot
yellow of this insect
on a vine; yet still may laud
what keeps our seasons
from degrading into shards.

WHAT IS IT DIES TODAY

All laws blown off like leaves
cold hate glides down the streets
misrule usurps routine
gross insults turd up speech
no fact seems safe to state
bland lies smear every screen
mean crowds chant gangster words
while children drown in reach

wild anger poisons friends
restraint's gone back to bed
the sky turns dark then red
the demon claws his prey
his minions get their way

what is it dies today

WORLD TRADE TWO
I will show you fear in a handful of dust.

First, it was the small things: Piled kicked-
off shoes in the street. A crusted thumb perched
curbside like a coin dropped on edge.
Racked portraits on poles, miming
saints-day processions. *The birds
fell off the roof*, the children said;
the birds were on fire.

Always it's the small things: A flight
of paper bellied on giant breaths,
flapping like bleached crows—
certificates of deposit paid in
dust. Ash trees turned ash.
Rasped breaths, as of shears, that
scissored the air.

Ever, it's the small things: dull thuds like
orchards lashed by gusts; a gingham doll
sprawled smiling, stiff with grime;
a stench that shut down nostrils and
clamped minds: *after*—after the avalanche its
boiling ten-league leaps, roar
muffling as earth.

Please let it be small things,
the shadows not the source.
For they are our sidelong glance
that sees while not seeing:
our chimneys, our moldering camps,
our warehouses of plaited hair
our metaphor

Mike Levin has been writing creatively all his adult life, legal deadlines notwithstanding. He holds degrees from the University of Pennsylvania, Harvard Law School, and Oxford (U.K.), where he was a Thouron Fellow. Chased by a Vietnam-era draft board, he declined playwriting fellowships to Carnegie and Yale Drama Schools, likely saving American theater. He has been published in over 50 periodicals or anthologies and has received poetry and feature journalism awards. His collections *Watered Colors* and *Man Overboard* were listed as *Best Poetry Books* for May 2014 and December 2018 by *Washington Independent Review of Books*. His third collection, *Falcons*, appeared in 2020.

Before entering private practice and becoming a renewable energy developer Mike served as an appellate lawyer, counselor and policy executive in several federal agencies; in the Carter White House as Deputy Director of a Cabinet-level Task Force; and as legislative aide to former Rep. Andrew Maguire (D-NJ) and the late Sen Edward M. Kennedy (D-MA). He was awarded the U.S. Environmental Protection Agency's Gold Medal for Exceptional Service (1982) and was an EPA nominee (1985) for the National Public Service Awards. A contributing editor to *BioCycle Magazine* and past contributing writer to the *Pennsylvania Gazette*, he has been listed in *Who's Who in American Law, Who's Who in Business and Finance*, and *Who's Who in the World*.

Milton Keynes UK
Ingram Content Group UK Ltd.
UKHW011545310124
437030UK00004B/177

9 798888 383629